FORECASTING ZERO:
U.S. NUCLEAR HISTORY AND THE
LOW PROBABILITY OF DISARMAMENT

The first half of the 20th century was replete with disarmament initiatives, including the Versailles Treaty, the Five-Power Treaty on Naval Disarmament, and the World Conference on Disarmament. Indeed, "[a]lmost every advance in weaponry, from the cross-bow to the bomber, has been accompanied by calls for the weapon's abolition."[1] In this sense, nuclear weapons have fared similarly to their predecessors.

Anti-nuclear weapon sentiment in the United States extends back at least as far as the days of the Manhattan Project. Some physicists, including German refugee Max Born, were so disgusted by the thought of atomic weapons that they refused to work on the Project at all. Others such as Leo Szilard joined the wartime effort but hoped that nuclear weapons would be used only as a deterrent against a potential Nazi nuclear weapon.

By contrast, key U.S. policymakers warmed early to the prospect of gaining a decisive military tool. President Franklin D. Roosevelt ordered the initiation of the Manhattan Project and was allegedly committed to using the bomb once ready, and President Harry S. Truman would eventually order the attacks on Hiroshima and Nagasaki, Japan. The Franck Committee's 1945 report, which warned of the consequences of nuclear use against Japan, and entreaties against nuclear use by leading scientists during the Roosevelt and Truman administrations, did little to derail this pro-nuclear wartime mood in Washington.[2]

To be sure, there was some disagreement in policy circles over the need to drop atomic weapons on Japan, including from then-General Dwight Eisenhower.[3] Yet there was little dissent over whether the United States should develop and possess them. Secretary of War Henry Stimson suggested that the bomb constituted a "royal straight flush" in favor of U.S. power. Secretary of State James Byrnes concurred that "the bomb might well put us in a position to dictate our terms at the end of the war." By May 1945, 1 month prior to release of the Franck Commission report, a decision had been made to use the bomb against Japan.[4]

Support for the bombing of Hiroshima and Nagasaki was widespread in the immediate aftermath of those attacks. Following the war, more than 86 percent of Americans polled viewed the attacks as legitimate.[5] With the exception of pacifists, some religious figures, and a few scientists, objections to the use and continued possession of nuclear weapons after the war appear to have been subsumed by a general desire to ensure a rapid Allied victory, as well as by hopes of favorably shaping the postwar global order.[6]

Shaping the Post-War World.

Interestingly, this same desire to shape the postwar world, in combination with a growing realization that nuclear technology was likely to spread, may have helped generate the first serious U.S. endorsement of disarmament. Thus, at the same time that President Truman was setting the stage for America's nuclear arms buildup, he and his administration were also attempting to establish domestic and international institutions to address the problem of nuclear control.[7]

Until 1949, the goal of disarmament was front and center among the Truman administration's nuclear policy initiatives. In November 1945, Truman, along with British Prime Minister Clement Attlee and Canadian Prime Minister William King, issued a joint communiqué explicitly supporting the "elimination of atomic energy for destructive purposes."[8] Shortly after the establishment of the United Nations Atomic Energy Commission (UNAEC) on January 24, 1946, the same Secretary of State James Byrnes, who had expressed support for the bomb during the war and who was attempting to diplomatically leverage the U.S. nuclear monopoly to gain advantage over the Soviets, created a special advisory committee charged with composing a report on atomic energy control. That committee's findings, better known as the Acheson-Lilienthal report, was to be submitted by the U.S. Government to the UNAEC. Presented to Secretary Byrnes in March, Acheson-Lilienthal did not set a date for U.S. nuclear disarmament, but it did express strong support for this goal.[9]

Yet Truman feared U.S. disarmament, absent guarantees that the Soviet Union's bomb-making potential would be neutered. In the shadow of chilling relations with the Soviets, he appointed Bernard Baruch as the American delegate to the UNAEC 1 day before Acheson-Lilienthal was to be submitted to it. Baruch proceeded to alter key elements of Acheson-Lilienthal in a way that addressed Truman's fears. He presented UNAEC with a plan that would have guaranteed U.S. disarmament, but only after the effective establishment of international controls. The Soviets rejected the plan, on the basis that it would have formally legitimized a temporary U.S. nuclear monopoly. When Baruch's plan failed during a UNAEC vote on December 30, 1946, the first era of U.S. disarmament efforts came to a close.[10] Indeed, serious efforts toward nuclear abolition would not return to the international agenda until late in the Cold War.[11]

Three Important Shifts Move the United States Away from Disarmament.

Though the intervening years were not marked by the complete absence of pro-disarmament sentiment in the United States, three important developments undermined the practical hopes of achieving abolition after the failure of the Baruch plan. First, the political situation changed. By 1949, the Truman Doctrine had been issued and the North Atlantic Treaty Organization (NATO) had been established to contain and counter the Soviet threat. In the shadow of growing antagonism and rapidly declining trust between the United States and the Soviets, the disarmament agenda was increasingly appropriated for propagandistic purposes, all but guaranteeing that no serious progress could be made toward the goal. Limited American efforts to advance disarmament by the newly elected Eisenhower administration were quickly rebuffed by Soviet leaders, whose intense focus on secrecy led them to reject the American insistence on conducting on-site verifications. Moscow instead insisted on complete disarmament without verification.[12]

Second, the birth of the nuclear arms race in 1949 dramatically altered the security situation. Thus, while the United States would enjoy a significant nuclear advantage over the Soviet Union for many years to come and while perceptions of a rapidly growing nuclear threat prompted President Eisenhower to call for the elimination of "atomic materials for military purposes," the emergence of a new and formidable enemy gave impetus to a growing perception in Washington that a political victory against communism required military strength, not disarmament.[13] Along these lines, the Eisenhower administration rejected Truman's distinction between nuclear and conventional weapons, embarking instead on an ultimately unsuccessful decade-long campaign to legitimize nuclear weapons as weapons like any other.[14] The 1950s also saw the implementation of Eisenhower's "New Look" policy which, driven by economic and military considerations, increased America's reliance on nuclear arms. These developments are captured well in Eisenhower's October 1953 doctrinal guidance that "[i]n the event of hostilities, the United States will consider nuclear weapons to be as available for use as other munitions."[15]

The third major change that undermined disarmament efforts was what seems to have been an emerging consensus among U.S. elites that America needed to refocus its attention on two more proximate and pressing matters: controlling an emerging arms race with the Soviets, and containing the global spread of atomic energy technology.[16] The shift toward arms control was particularly consequential, since there is a fundamental tension between policies centered on arms control and those centered on disarmament. By definition, disarmament changes the nature of the military balance, whereas most forms of arms control (e.g., arms reductions, limitations, and test bans) are directed at stabilizing an existing situation. This may be in part why Thomas Schelling once quipped that ". . . hardly anyone who takes arms control seriously believes that zero is the goal."[17] At any rate, creating a stable balance between the United States and the Soviet Union became an overriding concern of American policymakers throughout the next several decades. Some hoped that by stabilizing this balance and regulating nuclear energy transfers, the stage might be set for a gradual transformation of East-West relations and, eventually, disarmament.[18] But this goal remained consistently out of reach over the coming decades.

From Kennedy to Carter: The Rise of Arms Control.

U.S. officials continued to offer rhetorical and personal support for disarmament throughout the arms buildups of the 1960s and 1970s. In 1961, for example, President John Kennedy argued before the UN General Assembly that:

> The weapons of war must be abolished before they abolish us. . . . Men no longer maintain that disarmament must await the settlement of all disputes—for disarmament must be a part of any permanent settlement. And men may no longer pretend that the quest for disarmament is a sign of weakness—for in a spiraling arms race, a nation's security may well be shrinking even as its arms increase.[19]

By 1962, Kennedy had resumed disarmament negotiations with the Soviets, authorizing a three-step disarmament plan that would founder during the 1962-63 Geneva disarmament conference.[20] Indeed, there is no doubt that Presidents Kennedy and Lyndon Johnson, as well as leading members of their administrations such as Secretary of Defense Robert McNamara and Secretary of State Dean Rusk, harbored military and moral opposition to the use of nuclear weapons, and that they feared nuclear war.[21] Perceiving that continued increases in nuclear arms would produce little in the way of security gains, these policymakers took actions to stem the U.S.-Soviet arms race and establish international nonproliferation controls—efforts that led to the ratification of the 1968 Nuclear Nonproliferation Treaty (NPT) and the 1972 Strategic Arms Limitation Talks (SALT-I) under President Richard Nixon.[22] Article VI of the NPT embodied a commitment by nuclear-weapon states to work toward the elimination of their arsenals.

Notwithstanding policymakers' personal sentiments and incremental progress toward establishing greater nuclear controls, however, the prospects for disarmament became more remote during the 1960s and 1970s. First, Article VI of the NPT contained no metrics or timetable for disarmament. Second, Kennedy's 1962 disarmament proposal focused far more on near-term arms limitations than on eventual disarmament, and SALT-I similarly focused on stabilizing the East-West arms competition instead of eliminating the weapons. These facts demonstrated that the logic of arms control and nonproliferation, not of disarmament, had come to dominate the nuclear narrative among the superpowers. Third, perceptions of the structural situation prompted policymakers to build their arsenals to absurdly high numbers. Only one year before conclusion of the NPT, for example, the U.S. nuclear weapons stockpile had reached its peak of 32,000 warheads.[23] Any expressions of support for disarmament by U.S. policymakers during these years must be viewed in the context of these stunning increases, in both the quantity and quality of America's arsenal.

Not even the occasional burst of popular support for disarmament was enough to force the government's hand. To be sure, the disarmament movement enjoyed some successes: It helped push the U.S. Government toward adopting a nuclear test moratorium in 1958, and toward ratifying the Partial Test Ban Treaty (PTBT) and the NPT. Indeed, the disarmament movement arguably helped create the structural conditions for the administrations of Presidents Eisenhower, Kennedy, Johnson, Nixon, Gerald Ford, and Jimmy Carter to pursue various arms control initiatives.[24] The movement was similarly instrumental in opposing the B-1 bomber and the so-called neutron bomb,[25] and contacts between disarmament advocates and presidential candidate Jimmy Carter clearly influenced Carter's policy positions before he assumed office.[26] Evidence of this can be found in an October 1976 article of Carter's in the *Bulletin of the Atomic Scientists*, in which he explicitly links the legitimacy of nonproliferation efforts to progress toward disarmament. Carter wrote:

> I believe we have little right to ask others to deny themselves such weapons for the indefinite future unless we demonstrate meaningful progress toward the control, then reduction and, ultimately, elimination of nuclear arsenals.[27]

But the impact of the popular disarmament movement that had begun in 1945 was often constrained by popular fear of the Soviets and suspicions that the disarmament agenda was a communist plot—particularly with respect to its ultimate goal.[28] With the 1979 Soviet invasion of Afghanistan, the end of détente, the 1979 Iranian Revolution, and the taking of American hostages at the U.S. Embassy in Tehran, even the limited arms control achievements that the movement had helped bring about became suspect. Such events reminded Americans of the dangers beyond their shores and helped usher into office a tough-talking, anti-SALT President who would at first increase East-West tensions but ultimately help place disarmament back on the U.S. agenda as a primary policy goal.

A Reagan-era Rebirth for Disarmament.

It is both ironic and not at all so that by the end of Ronald Reagan's tenure, disarmament had regained a prominence on the U.S. agenda not seen since the failure of the Baruch Plan. The irony of the matter rests in the fact that when Reagan assumed office, his administration dragged the previous 2 decades of nuclear weapons policy decidedly rightward. Rather than attempting to rekindle an arms control process left teetering after the failure of SALT-II, Reagan up-ended the principle of strategic parity enshrined in the Anti-Ballistic Missile (ABM) Treaty and SALT-I by launching his Strategic Defense Initiative (SDI). He placed a particular focus on strategic modernization efforts, including pursuit of the MX Peacekeeper and Trident missiles, the B-1 strategic bomber, and cruise missile programs. The Reagan administration also changed the doctrinal thrust of nuclear weapons, planning to include not only deterrence but the fighting of both limited and prolonged nuclear wars. In fact, both he and his subordinates insisted in 1981 that any efforts to pursue arms control would have to wait until new weapons programs had progressed enough to give the United States leverage in negotiations.[29]

The return of disarmament during Reagan's tenure was also ironic because in moving away from arms con-

9

trol and deterrence, he unwittingly tapped into public fears about nuclear war that led to a shift in the political opportunity structure. This shift, in turn, ended up placing pressure on the Reagan administration to seek far-reaching accord with the Soviets on nuclear matters. The tenor and substance of his administration's early nuclear policies, for example, provoked considerable public unease and led to a previously unseen outpouring of support for anti-nuclear protests in the United States and Europe. With millions of people demonstrating in European capitals against proposed NATO nuclear deployments, the "nuclear freeze" movement gained momentum in the United States.[30] Popular culture became increasingly sympathetic to abolitionist sentiment through such publications as Jonathan Schell's *The Fate of the Earth* and the National Conference of Catholic Bishops' October 1982 moral critique of deterrence policy.[31] Elite doubts about the efficacy of deterrence and utility of nuclear weapons also began to emerge with greater force.[32] Such developments produced reluctance in Congress, even among some Republicans, to fund Reagan's defense programs, unless progress was made on the arms control front. By late 1982, public and congressional pressure led Reagan to initiate Strategic Arms Reduction Talks (the practical successor to SALT-II) and the Intermediate Nuclear Forces (INF) discussions.[33] These initiatives were much farther reaching than the SALT agreements because their goal was, for the first time, a reduction in the number of nuclear weapons possessed by the superpower rivals.

Yet, the return of disarmament during Reagan's tenure is not entirely ironic. President Reagan long held anti-nuclear sentiments, after all, beliefs that were rooted in his liberal past and religious convictions.[34] Thus, despite offering justifications of his administration's early hawkish policies, as early as 1982 one also finds Reagan suggesting in a radio address that "a nuclear war cannot be won and must never be fought."[35] He would repeat and expand upon this sentiment in a direct appeal to the Soviet people during his 1984 State of the Union address. Directly suggesting his desire for abolition, Reagan said:

> People of the Soviet Union, there is only one sane policy, for your country and for mine, to preserve our civilization in this modern age: A nuclear war cannot be won and must never be fought. The only value in our two nations possessing nuclear weapons is to make sure they will never be used. But then would it not be better to do away with them entirely?[36]

By the October 1986 U.S.-Soviet Reykjavik summit, Soviet Premier Gorbachev had also expressed support for eliminating all nuclear weapons, publicly presenting an ambitious plan to achieve this goal in 15 years. Gorbachev's heartfelt support of abolition, which he pursued at the summit, struck a chord with Reagan, lowering some of the trust-related structural barriers to cooperation, and resulting in perhaps the first serious discussion of the subject since the failure of the Baruch Plan.[37] Both leaders attempted to capitalize on the moment. Indeed, were it not for disagreements over the implications of the ABM Treaty for SDI, Reagan and Gorbachev might have reached an agreement to mutually disarm, an outcome that just days before the summit had been all but unthinkable among U.S. policymakers.[38] Although a formal agreement eluded the leaders at Reykjavik, Reagan and Gorbachev reached an oral agreement that their two countries should eliminate all nuclear weapons, with Reagan saying that "It would be fine with me if we eliminated all nuclear weapons," and Gorbachev replying that "We can do that."[39]

SHAPING A NEW WORLD ORDER, OR SHAPED BY IT? FROM REYKJAVIK TO ROGUE STATES

Looking back on Reykjavik, two things become clear. First, President Reagan spontaneously presided over and almost secured an agreement on nuclear disarmament. This highlights the tremendous importance of elite agency in what tends to be the highly bureaucratic realm of nuclear weapons policy.[40] Second, with public support for disarmament at an all-time high, with a mobilized public, with elites increasingly questioning the practical utility of nuclear weapons and the efficacy of deterrence strategy, and with U.S.-Soviet relations thawing, the structural situation was changing favorably for disarmament. Many of the obstacles that had prevented serious movement in that realm seemed to be fading away. The new phase of arms control marked by deep reductions (e.g., the INF and Strategic Arms Reduction [START] Treaty[41]), effectively "broke the back of the nuclear arms race."[42] One might even say that "the nuclear Cold War effectively ended in October 1986."[43] The goal of abolition appeared to be within reach.

New Risks and Uncertain Priorities in the Post-Cold War World (1991-2001).

For a brief period of time, it appeared that U.S. and Soviet leaders were reaching for this goal. Dramatic arms reductions captured headlines. The two superpowers' intermediate-range nuclear forces were completely eliminated through the 1987 INF treaty. The Presidential Nuclear Initiatives of 1991 and 1992, reciprocal but unilateral arms reductions, resulted in the withdrawal from service by the United States and the Soviet Union/Russia of as many as 17,000 tactical nuclear weapons. Ratified in 1991, the START-I treaty prompted not only further reductions, but increased transparency. Gone were the days when a paranoid Soviet state refused to accept verification, a point that had decades before dealt a mortal blow to disarmament.

Perhaps most consequentially, the Soviet Union had crumbled, dividing into 15 sovereign states. The Warsaw Pact's demise soon followed, and a lonely Russia entered a prolonged phase of economic decline and social instability. Further, by the end of the George H. W. Bush administration, a revolution in military affairs—specifically, the development of advanced conventional capabilities—had provided the United States with an overwhelming conventional military advantage against all potential adversaries.[44] Such developments left the United States in an unparalleled position of global dominance, one in which it could begin to shape a "new world order."[45]

Part of this new world order could have included a movement toward nuclear disarmament. Many of the cards *seemed* to be in place—decades of presidential support, continued commitment to Article VI, increasing fears of proliferation, the collapse of the Soviet threat and a relatively weak Russia, and an invigorated anti-nuclear movement. But the other shoe never dropped. Why, with the end of the Cold War, did disarmament largely fall off the political radar? Why did the Soviet collapse on the heels of Reykjavik fail to bring abolition to its logical conclusion?

One might offer numerous explanations for why disarmament stalled in the early 1990s, but at least five factors stand out. First, as the Soviet Union crumbled, U.S. policymakers turned to a variety of other matters—including the 1991 Gulf War, the Madrid peace conference, the reunification of Germany and, eventually, the expansion of NATO. Second, in the absence of an arms race, the popular movement that had swept the world during the 1980s largely lost its urgency. Third, fears of nuclear war with the Soviet Union transformed over time into fears of "loose nukes" and horizontal proliferation, all of which centered on the concern that "rogue" states or terrorist organizations would acquire nuclear weapons. This led to a gradual shift in U.S. policy focus away from arms reductions and disarmament, a shift that was perhaps best embodied by the elimination of the Arms Control and Disarmament Agency (ACDA) as an independent entity in April 1999, when the nearly 40-year old ACDA was fully merged into the U.S. Department of State.[46] Though U.S. officials continued to speak periodically about disarmament as a long-term goal, there were no well-structured or concerted efforts by them in the decade after the Cold War to achieve this goal. Indeed, by late 2005, another round of government reorganization had not only merged the State Department's Bureau of Arms Control with its Nonproliferation Bureau, but it had even resulted in the removal of the words "arms control" from the name of the Department's newly created Bureau of International Security and Nonproliferation.

Fourth, initial attempts to adapt the U.S. nuclear posture to meet new threats encountered heavy bureaucratic resistance, which ultimately resulted in a perpetuation of the status quo.[47] Finally, U.S. policymakers grew increasingly divided over how the sole remaining superpower should define and address the new international strategic context, as well as the role that America's nuclear weapons should play in this context. Were nuclear weapons still relevant for deterring past or emerging adversaries? Were they still relevant to extended deterrence commitments? Were they useful for dissuading states or terrorists from acquiring or using weapons of mass destruction (WMD)?[48] With the new millennium approaching, President Bill Clinton's Secretary of State, Madeleine Albright, poignantly observed that "the administration and Congress have not yet agreed on a common post-Cold War strategy for responding to [the development and proliferation of advanced nuclear weapons]."[49]

Thus, as Janne Nolan has argued, ". . . it is now a cliché in Washington that the end of the ideological struggle with the Soviet Union was not necessarily good news."[50] The predictable days (or at least they seemed so in retrospect) of the bipolar rivalry had ended. In their place had arrived strategic uncertainty. While arms control would enjoy some success during the Bush and Clinton administrations (e.g., START-I, the Lisbon Protocol, the Open Skies Treaty, the Agreed Framework, and START-II), and while the NPT was indefinitely extended in 1995, the United States would neither reach nor ratify many agreements after the early 1990s. Instead, in the absence of strong public interest in arms control or disarmament, uncertainty of how to adapt to the post-Cold War world, and with congressional and bureaucratic resistance to arms control initiatives and growing suspicion of Russia, initiatives such as the Comprehensive Test Ban Treaty (CTBT), the Fissile Material Cutoff Treaty (FMCT), and a third round of START floundered.[51] A nuclear posture review launched by President Clinton in 1993 and completed in 1994 seemed to reflect this trend. Rather than reducing America's reliance on nuclear weapons,

> The decisions that emerged from the 1993-94 Nuclear Posture Review. . . reinforced the operational and political importance of nuclear weapons. Taken together, these decisions ratified a triad of nuclear forces, with diminished but still large numbers of strategic forces; renewed the U.S. commitment to initiate the use of nuclear weapons against existing and potential new adversaries; and granted political approval for targeting plans to develop nuclear options against regional and nonnuclear contingencies.[52]

A 1997 Presidential Decision Directive providing guidance for nuclear weapons employment (PSS/NSC 60), the first such directive in over 15 years, similarly called for retaining a wide range of survivable nuclear options—from the ability to inflict overwhelming damage against enemy assets to more graduated options.[53]

Although U.S. policy failed to come into greater fundamental accord with broad disarmament goals, some American elites expressed a contrary view. Seeing the evolving situation differently, they believed that the Soviet collapse made abolition more, not less, important. A panel of experts brought together by the Stimson Center in Washington, DC, for example, argued in a 1995 report that the growing proliferation threat necessitated abolition on national security grounds. The recommendations of this panel, however, largely fell on deaf ears—even though its members included General Andrew Goodpaster and Paul Nitze, neither of whom could be considered shrinking national security violets.[54] A similar fate would befall a paper authored by the well-respected chairman of the House Armed Services Committee, Les Aspin, as well as a formal statement in favor of abolition by 58 generals and admirals, including 16 from the United States.[55]

To be sure, the United States had not suddenly lost its formal or rhetorical commitment to the goal of disarmament. The NPT's Article VI commitment was still in place, after all, and President Clinton from time to time highlighted it as the overarching U.S. goal. In March 2000, Clinton argued that:

> Remarkable progress in nuclear disarmament has occurred since the end of the Cold War. . . . The United States is committed to the ultimate elimination of all nuclear weapons. Achieving this goal will be neither easy nor rapid. Accordingly, the United States rededicates itself to work tirelessly and expeditiously to create conditions that will make possible even deeper reductions in nuclear weapons, and ultimately their elimination.[56]

But Clinton's assertion that the CTBT and other initiatives were steps toward disarmament is colored both by the lack of his articulation of a far-reaching disarmament strategy and the reality of a Nuclear Posture Review (NPR) and a Presidential Decision Directive (PDD) that maintained the centrality of nuclear weapons in U.S. security planning. Clinton's "lead and hedge" strategy against the possibility of a resurgent Russia or threats elsewhere, and his continuation of the Bush administration's policy of "calculated ambiguity," were practical manifestations of this continued centrality for nuclear weapons in U.S. policy.[57] Secretary of Defense William Cohen went so far as to suggest, in an interview with the *Washington Post*, that those who believed the end of the Cold War opened the door for a swift move toward U.S. nuclear abolition had no home in the Clinton administration.[58]

Disarmament Continues its Retreat (2001-09).

That the Clinton administration was not prepared to rush toward disarmament did not make it exceptional in the annals of American history. But this is exactly the point. While many U.S. administrations have expressed a desire for abolishing nuclear weapons, none has been willing to race toward the goal (not even when the structural conditions seemed most permissive), and almost none have articulated a clear view of and demonstrated a sustained commitment to disarmament—the George W. Bush administration perhaps least of all. Staffed by critics of traditional arms control approaches and abolition opponents, the Bush administration took a highly skeptical view toward international treaties and institutions generally.[59] The ascendant view in the halls of Washington, DC, in January 2001 was that treaties were not worth the paper they were written on, since states willing to sign treaties were often willing to take the actions required by them even in their absence. Further, this viewpoint held that American power could and should be used to further its foreign policy objectives. Those who would follow along were welcome; those who would not were "against us" and should be shunted aside.[60] These natural inclinations were exponentially magnified in the aftermath of the attacks of September 11, 2001 (9/11), which led administration officials to treat terrorism as the primary U.S. national security threat. Indeed, to the extent that the Bush administration focused on nuclear issues after 9/11, its efforts were primarily directed toward lowering the probability that a terrorist organization or a state sponsor of terrorism would acquire nuclear weapons, rather than toward concluding arms control agreements. None of this augured well for abolition.

These attitudes and events resulted in some significant departures from previous administrations' nuclear policies. One obvious departure was the Bush administration's disdain for old-style arms control treaties, with their intrusive and extensive verification provisions and strict limits on U.S. flexibility. Along these lines, the administration decided in 2001 to withdraw from the ABM Treaty in order to free itself from the legal shackles impeding development of a national missile defense (NMD) system — a reversal of 30 years of nuclear policy that contributed to significant deteriorations in U.S.-Russian relations.[61] The CTBT, widely thought to be a cornerstone of disarmament efforts, was left in legislative limbo — opposed both for its formality and lingering concerns about verifiability. In place of such agreements, a concerted effort was made to shift course in favor of less onerous treaties and informal agreements. Thus, while the Bush administration did conclude one significant arms reduction treaty with Russia in terms of numerical reductions — the 2002 Strategic Offensive Reductions Treaty (SORT) — the agreement contained no verification provisions of its own.[62] The 2003 Proliferation Security Initiative (PSI), although an important initiative in its own right, was not a treaty at all, but an informal agreement by interested parties to stem the illegal flow of materials that could be utilized in WMD programs.[63]

Supporters of Bush-era policy might counter that the SORT Treaty led to large reductions in strategic forces, and that the Bush administration actually reduced the U.S. reliance on nuclear weapons through its enumeration of the so-called "new triad" in the 2001 NPR and 2006 *National Security Strategy*, which integrated nuclear and advanced conventional forces for the purposes of deterrence.[64] These points could be used to suggest that, in effect, the Bush administration continued the move toward deep reductions, and that the unfavorable optics of the situation were due to partisan political posturing.[65] There is a measure of truth to such statements. There was little new, after all, about President Bush's emphasis on the centrality of nuclear weapons for hedging against current and future threats.[66] Moreover, the move toward greater integration of advanced conventional capabilities in the U.S. deterrent did represent a diversification of U.S. deterrence policy.[67] But one should not take this line of argument too far.

Creating an expanded role for the U.S. conventional arsenal and reducing the overkill capability of U.S. nuclear forces is not akin to advocating abolition, even though some Bush administration officials occasionally alluded to it as such.[68] Such actions notwithstanding, therefore, the Bush administration evinced a clear move away from established disarmament goals. This is particularly evident when one reviews developments at the 2005 NPT Review Conference, where the United States not only distanced itself from the 1995 and 2000 Conference decisions on disarmament (e.g., the "thirteen steps") but intervened to have removed from a UN summit document references to nonproliferation and disarmament.[69] The move away from abolition is also evident in the Bush administration's rejection of verification provisions in arms control treaties. It is widely accepted, after all, that intrusive verification and tough enforcement are necessary components of any move toward zero.[70] Simply put: no verification, no disarmament.

The Bush administration even endeavored to rewrite nonproliferation rules by dividing proliferators into two groups — those who could be trusted with their nuclear weapons (India) and those who must be isolated or attacked for their real or suspected actions (Iraq, Iran, and North Korea). Although the United States and India jointly pledged in June 2005 to support nonproliferation, for example, the nuclear deal with India advanced by the Bush administration contained no provisions to constrain India's military nuclear program.[71] While it is eminently reasonable to suggest that a nuclear-armed Saddam Hussein would have posed a far greater threat than does a nuclear-armed India, the relevant point here is that the Bush administration seemed to consider disarmament a priority only insofar as it pertained to "rogue" states and the possibility of terrorist acquisition of nuclear weapons.[72] If there was a general lack of concern vis-à-vis Indian nuclear weapons, one might ask, could U.S. disarmament have been a priority?

A NEW CENTER OR A RETURN TO NORMALCY? THE FOUR HORSEMEN RIDE TO TOWN

Thus, with the Bush administration entering its final years, disarmament seemed further away than ever. Moreover, by 2007, the post-Cold War world had undergone some dramatic shifts that made structural conditions decidedly less favorable for abolition, even as they made abolition itself more urgent. North Korea had built and tested its own nuclear weapons. Iran continued to defy International Atomic Energy Agency (IAEA) and United Nations (UN) Security Council demands, and was increasingly suspected of pursuing a weapons program. The United States had further reified the role of nuclear weapons in its national security strategy and had pushed ahead with missile defense plans to counter Iran and North Korea, providing an incentive for Russia—which was already relying more heavily on nuclear weapons for certain missions—to further increase this reliance.[73] At the same time, the START-I agreement was nearing expiration, with no successor in sight, and the NPT seemed to be crumbling under the weight of violations by Iran and North Korea and circumventions with respect to India. Finally, with the United States strategically hobbled by wars in Iraq and Afghanistan and with its influence declining globally, American leaders no longer appeared to be in a position to reshape the world dramatically according to their desires, even should they again decide to pursue disarmament.

It was in this context that former Secretaries of State George Schultz, William Perry, and Henry Kissinger, along with former Senator Sam Nunn, published their 2007 *Wall Street Journal* op-ed calling for a world without nuclear weapons.[74] Their statements have not necessarily been unique as an example of bipartisan support for abolition, since such support has never divided evenly along partisan lines.[75] More interesting is that these former Cold Warriors appear to have had a significant change of heart with respect to the nuclear question, and that their arguments are, unlike most previous efforts, gaining political traction in the United States. Not content to write opinion pieces, the so-called "four horsemen" have been actively engaging in efforts to build institutional and elite-level support for disarmament. Their boldness has helped not only to reintroduce abolition into the mainstream (albeit still as a long-term goal) but to set off a firestorm of debate among American elites about how to get to "global zero."

One interesting question that suggests itself here concerns why the "gang of four's" efforts have been so consequential in elevating discussions of abolition in the United States. This is not the first time that hawkish foreign policy and security luminaries have endorsed abolition.[76] A possible answer is that by 2007 the perceived urgency of disarmament had again grown, as nuclear weapons spread to troublesome actors and fears mounted that they would continue to spread — perhaps even into the hands of terrorists. Indeed, if one examines the logic behind the so-called gang of four's calls for abolition, a prime motivator seems to be that new nuclear states and terrorists may not be deterrable. With the threat of proliferation to such actors ever-present in a nuclear armed world, the four argue that nuclear weapons have become more of a liability than an asset for the United States.[77] Concerns over a recalcitrant Russia, the expiration of START-I verification provisions, and the weakening of the NPT may have similarly contributed to increasing the saliency of the pro-abolition argument among political elites. Perhaps the newfound excitement of elites over abolition also reflects a certain post-reactionary desire to correct course after the Bush administration's deviations from long-established norms.

FORECASTING THE U.S. NUCLEAR FUTURE: YES WE CAN (EVENTUALLY?)

The Obama Administration: Pledges and Actions.

It is commonly believed that the election of President Barack Obama has come at an opportune time, given the increasing pro-abolition sentiment of the past few years. Obama has consistently offered clear rhetorical support for a nuclear-free world—a deep conviction that he has held since his undergraduate days at Columbia University.[78] His most complete articulation of this vision was during an April 2009 speech at Hradcany Square in Prague, where he said that "today, I state clearly and with conviction America's commitment to seek the peace and security of a world without nuclear weapons."[79]

In addition to this personal commitment, one might also note that several leading Obama administration officials have publicly endorsed the vision of a nuclear-free world, including Robert Einhorn, Rose Gotemoeller, and Ivo Daalder.[80] Obama's combination of presidential statements and his choice of officials for top nuclear-related posts are perhaps the clearest indication that abolition has returned to the American political mainstream.[81] Indeed, the fact that disarmament is again a mainstream concept in the United States becomes particularly evident when one considers that during the 2008 presidential campaign, both then-Senator Obama and Senator John McCain—who agreed on little else—openly supported a prudent, step-wise movement toward disarmament.[82]

President Obama's words have been backed up with pledges to pursue several initiatives aimed at bringing disarmament closer to reality. Progress seems to be evident on multiple fronts. In September 2009, the President chaired a UN Security Council summit that unanimously approved the vision of a world without nuclear weapons.[83] The United States and Russia recently concluded a START follow-on agreement, New START, which mandates bilateral warhead and stockpile reductions and renews mechanisms for verification. The 2010 NPR, which was released in April 2010, reduces somewhat the role of nuclear weapons in U.S. strategy and foreign policy; indeed, throughout the deliberations over the NPR, the administration privately insisted on this outcome.[84] Also, in April 2010, the White House hosted a Nuclear Security Summit that brought together senior officials from 47 nations and won commitments for enhancing the safety and security of nuclear material, as well as for preventing nuclear smuggling and terrorism. Approximately 60 percent of national commitments made at this summit have been completed, and a follow-up summit is scheduled for 2012 in the Republic of Korea.[85]

Finally, the Obama administration's April 2010 conclusion of the New START agreement with Russia provided a strong foundation for reinvigorating the nonproliferation regime, which had been severely stressed after a decade of proliferation and political disagreements. Indeed, although state parties to the Nuclear Nonproliferation Treaty (NPT) had agreed in 1995 to extend the agreement indefinitely, the coming decade placed such strain on the nonproliferation regime that by 2005 the NPT Review Conference was unable to produce a final consensus document, due to disagreement over how to handle issues such as Iranian nuclear malfeasance and a Middle East Nuclear Weapon Free Zone. Non-nuclear weapon states (NNWS) had also become deeply skeptical that nuclear weapon states (NWS) were working in good faith to eliminate their nuclear arsenals, leading them to oppose strengthened nonproliferation activities without progress toward disarmament.

With the April 2010 signing of New START—the first new U.S.-Russian arms reduction treaty in nearly a decade—progress toward disarmament appeared to be restarted. Partly because of this progress, the 2010 NPT Review Conference was successful in producing a final document that included, among other things, a recommitment by NPT parties to the nonproliferation regime and an action plan on nonproliferation. Some believe that this positive outcome at the 2010 Review Conference had the ancillary benefit of strengthening the Obama administration's hand in dealing with both the Iranian and North Korean portfolios.[86]

Continuity, Not Revolution.

Despite this progress, however, the current pro-disarmament *zeitgeist* is not as revolutionary as it is sometimes portrayed. To be sure, nuclear disarmament debates in the United States may now be occurring in more detail and in a more sustained way than at most points in the past. But the step-wise, decades-long process advanced today by most advocates—one that begins with formalized arms reductions, a fissile material production cutoff, a comprehensive test ban, control over the nuclear fuel cycle, intense verification and enforcement, and gradual delegitimization of weapons possession, and that ends with abolition—is in many respects the very *same* approach that has been offered since the dawn of the nuclear age.

Moreover, previous presidents have enjoyed arms control and nonproliferation successes, and have

viewed their efforts as paving the way toward abolition. Yet, a variety of factors—from structural barriers to a lack of sustained political will—have impeded
progress toward that goal. Many of these factors continue to obstruct the path toward abolition. Indeed,
few mainstream proponents in the United States speak
of abolition as achievable anytime in the foreseeable
future. "I'm not naïve," said the President in Prague,
"This goal will not be reached quickly—perhaps not
in my lifetime."[87] If one makes the reasonable assump-
tion that, by modern standards of life expectancy,
President Obama could live at least another 40 years,
it becomes clear that the timeline envisioned by mainstream abolition supporters may be quite long—50,
60, 70, perhaps even 100 years or more.

Given all that might change in the interim, can
"such grand schemes . . . be carried forward by reasonable people making demonstrable progress at a
steady pace"?[88] Perhaps. Abolition is not on its face
unachievable, and the United States is not predestined
to sit atop a nuclear-armed world. Yet, numerous and
significant roadblocks to abolition linger. One might
divide these roadblocks into two broad categories:
conceptual and structural.

**Guarding Your Optimism: Conceptual Roadblocks
to Disarmament.**

The conceptual roadblock to disarmament might
be best illustrated by paraphrasing the classic film *Dr.
Strangelove*. Simply put, the United States has learned
to "love the bomb." Or better, one might describe it as
a love-hate relationship, one in which:

> Nuclear weapons are presented both as terrifying objects that could destroy the nation in half an hour and as the ultimate guarantors of our security. Nuclear weapons are terrifying, but deterrence keeps us safe.[89]

In short, Americans hate the bomb for what it can do to us and to innocent people worldwide, but we cherish it as the mainstay of our national security.[90] Learning, or perhaps more accurately, realistically planning and preparing to live without nuclear weapons, will be an important step toward abolition. Yet, this is a step that U.S. policymakers, including those in the Obama administration, have yet to take. This shortfall is reflected in the open-source literature on the subject, in which abolition proponents explore every conceivable question related to reaching global zero but are generally silent on how to achieve what may be the most difficult task of all—maintaining strategic stability while moving from low numbers to zero, as well as after arriving at zero.[91] Where these proponents do address the topic, they tend to suggest that, ultimately, what will be needed for "global zero" is a world in which the nature of international political relations is dramatically changed from what currently exists.[92] Such proposals can at times seem a bit fantastical, even for abolition supporters.

Indeed, the words and actions of the Obama administration suggest that nuclear deterrence will remain a cornerstone of U.S. national security for the foreseeable future, just as it has been for decades. Despite partisan attacks to the contrary, Obama is not a Pollyanna President.[93] He has stated unequivocally and in multiple venues, for example, that "As long as these weapons exist, the United States will maintain a safe, secure, and effective arsenal to deter any adversary, and guarantee that defense to our allies."[94] Vice President Joe Biden has similarly argued that this commitment will extend, "for as long as nuclear weapons are required to defend our country and our allies."[95] Their words have been backed up by actions; most recently, the administration has sought large funding increases for the U.S. nuclear weapons complex—a move that enjoyed bipartisan support from leading national security experts, including the so-called "gang of four" and the members of the Strategic Posture Commission, a bipartisan panel headed by former Defense Secretaries James Schlesinger and William Perry.[96]

Other administration officials have similarly emphasized the continuing importance of America's nuclear deterrent. In July 2009, Undersecretary of State for Arms Control Ellen Tauscher argued that while we need an "updated nuclear posture" that "more accurately reflect[s] the threat environment. . . . We must do this while continuing to deter any nuclear armed adversary and guarantee the defense of our allies."[97] It should be noted that Undersecretary Tauscher's comments were offered at a symposium on deterrence at the U.S. Strategic Command in Omaha, Nebraska. Also revealing is the language of the 2010 *Quadrennial Defense Review* (QDR), a document that simultaneously asserts that "new, tailored regional deterrence architectures" will permit "a reduced role for nuclear weapons in our national security strategy," and insists that:

> Until such time as the Administration's goal of a world free of nuclear weapons is achieved, nuclear capabilities will be maintained as a core mission of the Department of Defense. We will maintain a safe, secure, and effective nuclear arsenal to deter attack on the United States, and on our allies and partners.[98]

Even the strongest mainstream advocates of deep reductions and abolition seem to accept that the United States will need to maintain its nuclear deterrent for some time to come. Writers Hans M. Kristensen, Robert S. Norris, and Ivan Oelrich posit that:

> While the ultimate goal is nuclear abolition, a minimal deterrence doctrine creates a stable resting spot that minimizes the salience and danger of remaining nuclear weapons and allows all the world's nuclear powers to come into a stable equilibrium before moving to the last step of denuclearization.[99]

In short, mainstream abolition supporters may not be conceptually prepared for a nuclear-free world, even if it is technically possible to reach zero. Serious planning for maintaining security in a world with small numbers, and for doing so in a world with no nuclear weapons, must occur before the United States moves in that direction.[100] The ascendance of such discussions in the public sphere will be a better indication that the United States and the world are advancing significantly toward nuclear disarmament than talk of a second New START agreement, tactical weapon reductions, or movement toward ratifying the FMCT and CTBT.

Guarding Your Optimism: Structural Roadblocks to Disarmament.

While conceptual roadblocks provide partial insight into the U.S. nuclear future, structural roadblocks are at least as important to consider in this respect. During the Cold War, numerous structural barriers blocked the path toward disarmament. Even when the key structural barrier of East-West competition disintegrated with the end of the Cold War and the subsequent collapse of the Soviet Union, others took its place. What one finds today is a complex web of structural barriers to abolition, some of which have long pedigrees, some of which are relatively new. While structural permissiveness does not guarantee policy outcomes, these barriers will also need to be addressed if serious U.S. movement toward abolition is to be realized.

One such barrier is a byproduct of the material and human support afforded to the American nuclear infrastructure. Nuclear weapons-related programs continue to receive appropriations that dwarf a variety of other federal programs. In 2008, the United States spent more than $52.4 billion on nuclear weapons programs; Stephen I. Schwartz and Deepti Choubey write:

> By way of comparison, the 2008 nuclear weapons and weapons-related "budget" exceed[ed] all anticipated government expenditures on international diplomacy and foreign assistance ($39.5 billion) and natural resources and the environment ($33 billion). It is nearly double the budget for general science, space, and technology ($27.4 billion), and it is almost 14 times what the U.S. Department of Energy has allocated for all energy-related research and development.[101]

Reinforcing this commitment, the Obama administration has consistently supported increased funding for the U.S. nuclear complex and deterrent.[102] This budgetary support has been complemented by efforts to incentivize job assignments related to the nuclear deterrent, particularly in the wake of concerns that the nuclear weapons infrastructure is decaying, and of security fears emanating from high-profile mishaps of the past few years, including the unauthorized flight in 2007 of six nuclear-armed cruise missiles from Minot Air Force Base in North Dakota to Barksdale Air Force Base in Louisiana.[103]

Such efforts are largely aimed at ensuring the credibility and security of America's nuclear arsenal, an entirely reasonable objective so long as the United States possesses and relies on nuclear weapons. Yet, they may also have negative consequences with respect to abolition, including leading to a further entrenchment of the nuclear mission in U.S. security policy. The bureaucracies supported and reified by today's decisions are likely to prove resilient in the future as attempts are made to advance broad changes in nuclear policy such as abolition.[104] The case of the 1994 NPR is a good example of how bureaucracies are adept at resisting change.[105] Unsurprisingly, the Obama administration encountered significant bureaucratic resistance by "elements within the Department of Defense (DoD) and other agencies," during the writing of the 2010 NPR.[106]

A second structural barrier is the lack of public mobilization in favor of abolition. Unlike in previous decades, the most recent push for abolition is an elite-level phenomenon.[107] Gone are the days where millions marched in European capitals, and a "ban the bomb" movement swept the United States. The outrage, fear, and sense of urgency that drove public involvement in the nuclear issue—from the 1950s to the early 1990s—largely faded with the Cold War. Polling over the past 6 years underlines this shift. In 2007, only 38 percent of Americans (and 31 percent of Russians) agreed when asked if "our goal should be to gradually eliminate all nuclear weapons through an international agreement, while developing effective systems for verifying all countries are eliminating theirs too."[108]

While this polling was conducted before the latest push for abolition reached full stride, its results are still noteworthy. Since the question asked hews closely to abolition proponents' current proposals, including those of the Obama administration, the results demonstrate, at a minimum, the lack of public accord on what our nuclear future should be. Consider also that when asked the same question in 2004, 55 percent of Americans responded affirmatively that disarmament should be the end goal. This precipitous decline, coupled with minimal public interest in ratification of the New START Treaty in 2010, suggests that American political leaders are not likely to face much domestic pressure to act on disarmament over the coming years. The absence of such pressure is important, because research demonstrates that popular mobilization has been an important facilitator of substantive agreements on nuclear weapons use and possession—one that influences politicians through direct pressure by changing the political opportunity structure in which they operate.[109]

Indeed, it is hard to overstate the importance of domestic politics as a structural roadblock to disarmament, as was evidenced by the bitter debates over ratification of New START. Much to the surprise of the Obama administration and expert analysts, Senator Jon Kyl (R-AZ), the Republican point man on nuclear arms issues, led a protracted effort in opposition to the Treaty, despite having been granted many concessions by the administration. Moreover, whatever the ultimate reason for Senator Kyl's opposition—whether political or technical—legislative efforts continue in Congress to place limitations on New START implementation and delay reductions, efforts that could undermine the Treaty if enacted into law.[110] To be sure, the New START debates placed arms control back on the national stage and to an extent may have educated a new generation of congressional staff about these issues, but the lingering efforts in opposition to New START suggest that any follow-on arms control initiatives, let alone initiatives that would substantially advance the goal of disarmament, are likely to face stiff resistance on Capitol Hill.

Another structural barrier to Washington's decision to disarm is related to the conditions set by American policymakers for moving forward with abolition. Like others before him, President Obama clearly states that the United States will retain its deterrent "so long as there is a country with nuclear weapons."[111] The 2010 QDR insists that the DoD nuclear mission will be sustained "[u]ntil such time as the Administration's goal of a world free of nuclear weapons is achieved."[112] The "gang of four" argues that "as we work to . . . realize the vision of a world without nuclear weapons, we recognize the necessity to maintain the safety, security, and reliability of our own weapons."[113] One cannot help but think that this "you first" approach is strikingly similar to the Baruch plan's insistence that the United States will disarm only once others have done so. Yet, a U.S. nuclear monopoly is not likely to be any more acceptable to other states in the future than it was to the Soviets in the late 1940s.

These issues point to a fourth structural roadblock. Put in the interrogative: If U.S. disarmament depends on the disarmament of others, will those others disarm? Despite the increased talk about abolition over the past several years in Western capitals, global trend lines do not match the rhetoric. Russia is arguably increasing, not decreasing, its reliance on nuclear weapons; some observers believe that Moscow is in the process of increasing its nuclear arsenal. While Russian representatives deny this accusation, it nonetheless proved a major stumbling block at last year's Global Zero talks in Paris.[114] In the Middle East, Iran's blatant defiance of UN Security Council and IAEA demands underscores suspicions that it is pursuing a military nuclear capability. Faced with a potential nuclear-armed Iran and surrounded by largely hostile states, Israel is unlikely to disarm. More than 10 other Middle Eastern states are currently pursuing nuclear energy agreements with suppliers, cooperation that may be driven in part by fears of Iran and that could lead to future proliferation.[115]

A similar situation obtains elsewhere. Indo-Pakistani relations have improved somewhat over the past several years, but the two states remain adversaries and show no signs of reaching a groundbreaking nuclear or political accord. Reportedly, Pakistan has nearly doubled its nuclear arsenal over the past few years and continues to increase its production of fissile material. As a result, Islamabad may soon become the world's fifth largest nuclear power, ahead of Great Britain.[116] In East Asia, North Korea has already tested two weapons and, while it seems to be holding off on a third test, six-party efforts to promote a denuclearized Korean peninsula remain deadlocked. Even France, which is situated in peaceful and prosperous Western Europe, remains skeptical about disarmament. At the 2010 Paris disarmament talks, French Foreign Ministry Secretary General Pierre Sellal coyly offered that "France's nuclear deterrent has protected our country very well for many years."[117]

What events would be required to bring these states closer to disarmament? The potential list is long and notoriously difficult to achieve, including a halt to NATO expansion and U.S. involvement in Russia's "near-abroad," Arab-Israeli peace, and resolution of the Kashmir conflict. With respect to North Korea and Iran, the question is at least as complex, and would involve denuclearization of the Korean peninsula and bringing Iran into full compliance with IAEA and UN Security Council demands. Aside from the resolution of all of these conflicts, successful abolition might also require the establishment of an international norm against nuclear possession to undermine the legitimacy of those who may in the future seek to acquire or retain nuclear arsenals. The key point here is simply that a structural context favorable to disarmament looks little like the world in which we live today.

When discussing structural roadblocks to disarmament, one must also consider the role of the so-called power paradox. This concept describes a situation in which a huge conventional military advantage makes nuclear disarmament possible and perhaps even preferable for the United States, however, that same conventional advantage may simultaneously make other states less likely to disarm.[118] When weaker states look through the lens of the power paradox, they may see U.S. advocacy for disarmament as a cynical "ploy" aimed at consolidating American power rather than as a means toward establishing a safer world.[119] A forceful push for disarmament, in the context of overweening U.S. conventional dominance, could thus bring about an equally strong anti-disarmament reaction from states seeking to hedge against U.S. power.

Even if agreement is reached among states to move in tandem toward zero, there remains the challenge of establishing effective verification and enforcement of disarmament. Many states may be unwilling to accept intrusive verification inspections or, after accepting them, seek to circumvent them or renege on their commitments. North Korea's withdrawal from the NPT and the international community's impotence in dealing with it are particularly illustrative here, but so is the case of the United States under the Bush administration, since it not only withdrew from the ABM Treaty but willingly let agreements with important verification provisions expire. Provided that verification concerns are overcome, the challenge of enforcement will remain. To make restrictions effective, it must be possible to punish violators, but setting up an effective mechanism for doing so remains a difficult endeavor. One analyst has insisted that enforcement is "perhaps the greatest challenge in nuclear disarmament," noting that the difficulties associated with enforcement are highlighted by the cases of Iraq, North Korea, Iran, Libya, and Syria.[120]

Verification and enforcement are important not only with respect to the elimination of nuclear arsenals but to the spread of sensitive nuclear materials and technologies that can facilitate proliferation. International agreement on strong measures to secure the nuclear fuel cycle and nuclear materials generally would help to create a solid basis on which the United States and others could move toward disarmament. Yet, the challenges here are long-standing and substantial. The FMCT remains trapped in the UN Conference on Disarmament, even though there are efforts underway to find alternative venues for its consideration. The CTBT is unlikely to be ratified by all the states necessary for it to come into force at any point in the foreseeable future. Securing nuclear materials and preventing proliferation will likely also require internationalization of the nuclear fuel cycle, making the Additional Protocol (AP) a condition of nuclear supply, and banning the transfer of enrichment and reprocessing (ENR) technologies to any state that does not already possess them. Notwithstanding some progress on multilateral fuel cycle facilities, nuclear suppliers remain divided over whether to require the AP as a precondition for all types of nuclear assistance. Proposals to ban ENR transfers are even more divisive, with few besides the United States supporting them, and with Washington itself divided over the idea.

One must also consider the impact of future cases of proliferation on U.S. behavior, as well as the impact of these actions on the prospects for disarmament. The case of Iraq in 2003 is instructive here. While a majority of Americans were supportive of moves toward general nuclear disarmament during the initial period in which charges of WMD possession were leveled against Saddam Hussein, they seemed also to have been inclined to respond to this perceived threat through the use of military force, particularly in the wake of the 9/11 attacks and the history of conflict with Hussein's Iraq. Leaving aside the debate about the Bush administration's motivations for going to war in Iraq in 2003, the relevant point here is that aggressive responses to proliferation may heighten the salience of the power paradox—both in the target state and among observers—by highlighting the extent of U.S. conventional military superiority and the security fears of weaker U.S. adversaries. By extension, these responses also may make achieving disarmament more difficult. Consider, for example, that in December 2003, Libyan leader Muammar Gaddafi announced his decision to relinquish all elements of Libya's WMD program. In spring 2011, the United States and NATO launched military action against Gaddafi's forces in Libya under the banner of protecting civilian life. Future proliferators are likely to give careful consideration to the question of whether, if Gaddafi had retained his WMD program, NATO might have refrained from taking these actions. At the same time, there may also be risks to inaction in the face of weapons proliferation since, if proliferation is tacitly accepted, it may gradually weaken the nonproliferation regime and undermine one of the key institutional requirements for successful abolition.

A final structural roadblock to U.S. disarmament that must be considered is Washington's continued reliance on nuclear weapons as a cornerstone of its national defense, including its extended deterrent commitments to allies. This is more than a conceptual problem, because so long as nuclear weapons provide the central backstop for direct and extended deterrence, it will be practically impossible to eliminate them. Barring a dramatic reduction in the need for deterrence strategies, therefore, a prerequisite to U.S. disarmament will be the deployment of conventional alternatives that assuage fears about nuclear drawdowns held by U.S. policymakers and their allies, without antagonizing potential peer competitors such as Russia and China or exacerbating the power paradox.[121] The activation of the U.S. Global Strike Command in August 2009 represents some progress in the integration of advanced conventional capabilities in America's deterrent posture. Conventional Prompt Global Strike (PGS) may eventually help pave the way for a deep reduction in America's reliance on nuclear weapons; indeed, as other states reduce their nuclear arsenals, the efficacy of conventional capabilities for deterrence is likely to grow. But this efficacy will depend on foreign space- and cyber-warfare capabilities, since the effectiveness of PGS depends in large part on the security of computer networks and the availability of satellite guidance, and it is precisely those capabilities that are emerging as the major new threats to U.S. national security.

CONCLUSION

One might draw two tentative conclusions about America's nuclear future based on the present study. First, the Obama administration's advocacy of nuclear abolition and its efforts to move down this path are significant, but President Obama's support for disarmament is hardly a radical break from the past. Indeed, Obama's approach to the issue is overwhelmingly cautious in nature, reflecting as it does a widely shared view among American policymakers that, although disarmament is in the long-term American interest, it must not be pursued at the expense of near-term national security requirements. Moreover, substantial roadblocks remain on the path toward abolition. Some of these roadblocks will be particularly daunting to overcome and may require a dramatic evolution in the conduct and nature of international political relations. Thus, it is highly unlikely that Washington will make any bold moves toward global zero in the foreseeable future. A more probable outcome is that the Obama administration will continue to move in step-wise motion toward the long-term goal of abolition, a goal that the President acknowledges will not be achieved in our lifetimes.

The second broad conclusion one can draw is that history is an unpredictable handmaiden of events. Throughout the U.S. nuclear past, support for abolition as well as the barriers to it have ebbed, flowed, and transformed. Ironically, when the barriers to disarmament seemed lowest, political and popular enthusiasm for this goal largely dissipated. It may therefore be the case that when disarmament is most needed, it is least possible, and when it is most possible, it is least desired. Whether this trend will hold in the future, and what can be done to militate against it, remain open questions. If future administrations are less committed to nuclear disarmament, if elite and public support for abolition fails to coalesce, and if the strategic context shifts in unexpected ways, the current push for disarmament could be derailed.

What does the future hold for the abolitionist agenda? From American shores, the mission has regained prominence. But the answer is as unclear as it ever was.

ENDNOTES

1. Coit D. Blacker and Gloria Duffy, eds., *International Arms Control: Issues and Agreements*, 2nd Ed., Stanford, CA: Stanford University Press, 1984, p. 81.

2. Lawrence S. Wittner, *Confronting the Bomb: A Short History of the World Nuclear Disarmament Movement*, Stanford, CA: Stanford University Press, 2009, pp. 2-4; Blacker and Duffy, pp. 95-96. The Franck Committee's warnings included the possibility of an arms race with the Soviets and an inability to control the further spread of nuclear weapons once used. See James Franck *et al.*, "Report of the Committee on Political and Social Problems, Manhattan Project 'Metallurgical Laboratory' of the University of Chicago," Franck Report, June 11, 1945, available from *www.nuclearfiles.org/ menu/key-issues/ethics/issues/scientific/franck-report.htm*.

3. Wittner, *Confronting the Bomb*, p. 6; Nina Tannenwald, "Stigmatizing the Bomb: Origins of the Nuclear Taboo," *International Security*, Vol. 29, No. 4, 2005; Nina Tannenwald, "The Nuclear Taboo: The United States and the Normative Basis of Nuclear Non-Use," *International Organization*, Vol. 53, No. 3, 1999.

4. Wittner, *Confronting the Bomb*, p. 4.

5. Paul Boyer, *Fallout: A Historian Reflects on America's Half-Century Encounter with Nuclear Weapons*, Columbus, OH: Ohio State University Press, 1998, p. 25.

6. Lawrence S. Wittner, *One World or None: A History of the World Nuclear Disarmament Movement Through 1953, Vol. 1: The Struggle against the Bomb*, Stanford, CA: Stanford University Press, 1993. On the shaping of the post-war order according to U.S. preferences, see G. John Ikenberry, *After Victory: Institutions, Strategic Restraint, and the Rebuilding of Order After Major Wars*, Princeton, NJ: Princeton University Press, 2001.

7. Tannenwald, "Stigmatizing the Bomb," p. 17. On how Truman administration actions contributed to a nuclear arms build-up, see Blacker and Duffy, pp. 96-99; David Alan Rosenberg, "The Origins of Overkill: Nuclear Weapons and American Strategy, 1945-1960," *International Security*, Vol. 7, No. 4, 1983.

8. Harry S. Truman, C. R. Attlee, and W. L. Mackenzie King, "Declaration on Atomic Energy by President Truman and Prime Ministers Attlee and King," *United States Treaties and Other International Acts Series*, No. 1504, November 15, 1945, available from *www.ibiblio.org/pha/policy/post-war/451115b.html*. The language of the communiqué was drafted by Vannevar Bush, then the director of the Office of Scientific Research and Development. See Tannenwald, "Stigmatizing the Bomb," p. 20.

9. Large parts of this document were reportedly written by the former scientific head of the Manhattan Project, turned nuclear critic, Robert Oppenheimer. See Blacker and Duffy, p. 96; David Lilienthal *et al.*, "A Report on the International Control of Atomic Energy," Washington, DC: U.S. Government Printing Office, March 16, 1946, available from *honors.umd.edu/HONR269J//archive/AchesonLilienthal.html*; U.S. Department of State, "The Acheson-Lilienthal & Baruch Plans, 1946," U.S. Department of State Office of the Historian, Timeline of U.S. Diplomatic History, 1945-1952, nd.

10. "The Acheson-Lilienthal & Baruch Plans, 1946."

11. George Perkovich and James M. Acton, eds., *Abolishing Nuclear Weapons: A Debate*, Washington, DC: Carnegie Endowment for International Peace, 2009, p. 83.

12. George Bunn and John B. Rhinelander, "Reykjavik Revisited: Toward a World Free of Nuclear Weapons," *World Security Institute Policy Brief*, September 2007, p. 4; Blacker and Duffy, pp. 99-101.

13. The U.S. stockpile grew to about 200 in 1949, and drastically increased after the drafting of NSC 68 in 1950. Although the Soviet Union tested its first atomic bomb in 1949, at the time of Stalin's death the Soviets had only about 50 atomic bombs, a 17-to-1 disadvantage in favor of the United States. Yet, by 1953, each nation had developed the hydrogen bomb, and by 1955, each had the long-range bombers to deliver them. See Paul Rogers, "Learning from the Cold War Nuclear Confrontation," in Alan P. Dobson, ed., *Deconstructing and Reconstructing the Cold War*, Brookfield, UK: Ashgate, 1999, pp. 205-206; John Lewis Gaddis, *We Now Know: Rethinking Cold War History*, New York: Oxford University Press, 1997, pp. 102-103.

14. Tannenwald, "Stigmatizing the Bomb," pp. 18, 23-26; Blacker and Duffy, pp. 99-101; Dwight D. Eisenhower, "Address by Mr. Dwight D. Eisenhower, President of the United States of America, to the 470th Plenary Meeting of the United Nations General Assembly," December 8, 1953, available from *www.iaea.org/About/history_speech.html*.

15. McGeorge Bundy, "To Cap the Volcano," *Foreign Affairs*, Vol. 48, No. 1, 1969, p. 246.

16. Lawrence Freedman, "A New Theory for Nuclear Disarmament," *Bulletin of the Atomic Scientists*, Vol. 65, No. 4, 2009, p. 14; Bunn and Rhinelander, p. 4; William Walker, "Nuclear Enlightenment and Counter-enlightenment," *International Affairs*, Vol. 83, No. 3, 2007, p. 435. See also the Fall 1960 *Daedalus* special issue on arms control.

17. Thomas C. Schelling, "What Went Wrong with Arms Control," *Foreign Affairs*, Vol. 64, No. 2, 1985/86, p. 226.

18. Walker, "Nuclear Enlightenment and Counter-enlightenment," p. 437.

19. John F. Kennedy, "Address Before the General Assembly of the United Nations," September 25, 1961, available from *www.jfklibrary.org/Historical+Resources/Archives/Reference+Desk/Speeches/JFK/003POF03UnitedNations09251961.htm*.

20. Bunn and Rhinelander, p. 4.

21. Tannenwald, "Stigmatizing the Bomb," p. 29.

22. Glenn T. Seaborg and Benjamin T. Loeb, *Stemming the Tide*, Lexington, KY: Lexington Books, 1987, p. 197; Blacker and Duffy; Morton H. Halperin, "The Decision to Deploy the ABM: Bureaucratic and Domestic Politics in the Johnson Administration," *World Politics*, Vol. 25, No. 1, 1972; Bundy; Robert S. McNamara, "Mutual Deterrence," San Francisco, CA, September 18, 1967, available from *www.atomicarchive.com/Docs/Deterrence/Deterrence.shtml*.

23. Robert S. Norris and Hans M. Kristensen, "US Nuclear Warheads, 1945-2009," *Bulletin of the Atomic Scientists*, Vol. 65, No. 4, 2009, p. 73.

24. Jeffrey Knopf, *Domestic Society and International Cooperation: The Impact of Protest on US Arms Control Policies*, Cambridge, UK: Cambridge University Press, 1998; Blacker and Duffy, p. 115; Barry Blechman, "Do Negotiated Arms Limitations Have a Future?" *Foreign Affairs*, Vol. 59, No. 1, 1980, pp. 114-115. One must also take into consideration, however, that Johnson, Nixon, and Carter-era decisions to pursue arms control were made so in large part because administration officials thought the arms race destabilizing and were looking for ways to contain the Soviet threat. See Lawrence Freedman, *The Evolution of Nuclear Strategy*, 2nd Ed., New York: Palgrave Macmillan, 2003, pp. 338, 59-60; William Burr, "Sino-American Relations, 1969: The Sino-Soviet Border War and Steps Toward Rapprochement," *Cold War History*, Vol. 1, No. 3, 2001; Michael Krepon, "Moving Away From MAD," *Survival*, Vol. 43, No. 2, 2001, p. 82; Arnold Horelick, "US-Soviet Relations: The Return of Arms Control," *Foreign Affairs*, Vol. 63, No. 3, 1984, pp. 523-525.

25. Wittner, *Confronting the Bomb*, pp. 112-140; Lawrence S. Wittner, *Toward Nuclear Abolition: A History of the World Nuclear Disarmament Movement, 1971 to the Present*, Vol. 3 of *The Struggle Against the Bomb*, Stanford, CA: Stanford University Press, 2003, pp. 440-445.

26. Wittner, *Toward Nuclear Abolition*.

27. Jimmy Carter, "Three Steps Toward Nuclear Responsibility," *Bulletin of the Atomic Scientists*, Vol. 32, No. 8, 1976, p. 11.

28. Wittner, *Confronting the Bomb*, p. 112.

29. Schelling, p. 225; Blacker and Duffy, p. 272; Blechman, "Do Negotiated Arms Limitations Have a Future?"

30. Knopf; John Lofland, *Polite Protesters: The American Peace Movement of the 1980s*, Syracuse, NY: Syracuse University Press, 1993; Robert Kleidman, *Organizing for Peace: Neutrality, the Test Ban, and the Freeze*, Syracuse, NY: Syracuse University Press, 1993.

31. Jonathan Schell, *The Fate of the Earth*, New York: Knopf, 1982; National Conference of Catholic Bishops, "The Challenge of Peace: God's Promise and Our Response, a Pastoral Letter on War and Peace," Washington, DC, United States Catholic Conference, May 3, 1983.

32. David S. Yost, "The Delegitimization of Nuclear Deterrence," *Armed Forces and Society*, Vol. 16, No. 4, 1990; Edward Luttwak, "An Emerging Post-Nuclear Era," *Washington Quarterly*, Vol. 11, No. 1, 1988; Robert S. McNamara, "The Military Role of Nuclear Weapons: Perceptions and Misperceptions," *Foreign Affairs*, Vol. 62, No. 1, 1983.

33. Blacker and Duffy, p. 273.

34. Paul Lettow, *Ronald Reagan and His Quest to Abolish Nuclear Weapons*, New York: Random House, 2005.

35. Ronald Reagan, "Radio Address to the Nation on Nuclear Weapons," April 17, 1982, available from *www.presidency.ucsb.edu/ws/index.php?pid=42414*.

36. Ronald Reagan, "Address Before a Joint Session of the Congress on the State of the Union," Washington, DC, January 25, 1984, available from *www.presidency.ucsb.edu/ws/index.php?pid=4020.5*.

37. Some key structural barriers would arguably collapse in 1991 with the disintegration of the Soviet Union.

38. As a pre-Reykjavik memo from Secretary of State George Schultz to Reagan suggests, the United States did not expect that the summit would lead to an agreement at all, but rather that it would prepare the ground for a follow-up summit. See George Schultz, "Memorandum to the President, Subject: Reykjavik," October 2, 1986, available from *www.gwu.edu/~nsarchiv/NSAEBB/NSAEBB203/index.htm*.

39. Nikolai Sokov, "Reykjavik Summit: The Legacy and a Lesson for the Future," *NTI Issue Brief*, December 2007, available from *www.nti.org/e_research/e3_95.html*; Don Oberdorfer, *From the Cold War to a New Era: The United States and the Soviet Union, 1983-1991*, New York: Poseidon Press, 1991, p. 202.

40. See, for example, Janne Nolan, *An Elusive Consensus: Nuclear Weapons and American Security After the Cold War*, Washington, DC: Brookings Institution Press, 1999.

41. While work on START-I progressed during the Reagan administration, the agreement came into force under George H. W. Bush.

42. Michael Krepon, "Ban the Bomb. Really," *The American Interest*, Vol. 3, No. 3, 2008, p. 90.

43. Walker, "Nuclear Enlightenment and Counter-Enlightenment," p. 438.

44. Mary Kaldor, *New Wars, Old Wars: Organized Violence in the Global Era*, Stanford, CA: Stanford University Press, 1999.

45. Eli Corin, "Presidential Nuclear Initiatives: An Alternative Paradigm for Arms Control," *NTI Issue Brief*, 2004, available from *www.nti.org/e_research/e3_41a.html*; Freedman, *The Evolution*

of Nuclear Strategy, pp. 407-408. A brief point of clarification is in order here: President George H. W. Bush's famous reference to a "new world order" actually occurred in September 1990, prior to the Soviet collapse. Accordingly, he envisioned the Soviet Union as playing a role in this order. See *ibid.*, p. 408. I use the term here in a slightly different sense.

46. Susan B. Epstein, "State Department and Related Agencies: FY2001 Appropriations," *CRS Report for Congress*, Washington, DC: Congressional Research Service, February 13, 2001.

47. Nolan.

48. Wittner, *Confronting the Bomb*, Chap. 9; Freedman, *The Evolution of Nuclear Strategy*, pp. 409-410; Scott D. Sagan, "The Commitment Trap: Why the United States Should Not Use Nuclear Threats to Deter Biological and Chemical Weapons Threats," *International Security*, Vol. 24, No. 4, 2000; Nolan, pp. 1-5.

49. Madeleine Albright, "A Call for American Consensus: Why Our Arms Control Leadership is Too Important to Risk in Partisan Political Fights," *Time*, November 22, 1999. Albright was here specifically addressing the Senate's rejection of the CTBT. A potential alternative explanation for CTBT rejection not accounted for here is the extent to which a Republican Congress sought to deny President Clinton a political victory as he struggled with scandal at home.

50. Nolan, p. 2.

51. Walker, "Nuclear Enlightenment and Counter-enlightenment," pp. 438-440; Nolan, Chap. 5. If one considers that START II, though ratified during Clinton's term, was actually signed by President George H. W. Bush, this gap in progress is even more striking.

52. Nolan, p. 87.

53. The text of this document, as well as the 1994 NPR, remains highly classified. See "PDD/NSC 60, Nuclear Weapons Employment Policy Guidance," Washington, DC: U.S. National Security Council, November 1997, available from *fas.org/irp/off-docs/pdd60.htm*.

54. See Andrew J. Goodpaster *et al.*, "An Evolving US Nuclear Posture," Second Report of the Steering Committee, Project on Eliminating Weapons of Mass Destruction, Washington, DC: Henry L. Stimson Center Report, December 1995, available from *www.stimson.org/pdf/Report19.pdf*. Nitze would later echo his support for abolition in a *New York Times* op-ed. Nitze wrote:

> The technology of our arsenals is such that we can achieve accuracies of less than three feet from the expected point of impact. The modern equivalent of a stick of dynamite exploded within three feet of an object on or near the earth's surface is more than enough to destroy the target. In view of the fact that we can achieve our objectives with conventional weapons, there is no purpose to be gained through the use of our nuclear arsenal. To use it would merely guarantee the annihilation of hundreds of thousands of people, none of whom would have been responsible for the decision invoked in bringing about the weapons' use, not to mention incalculable damage to our natural environment . . . in the long term . . . it is the presence of nuclear weapons that threatens our existence.

See Paul Nitze, "A Threat Mostly to Ourselves," *New York Times*, October 8, 1999, available from *www.nytimes.com/1999/10/28/opinion/a-threat-mostly-to-ourselves.html?pagewan%20ted=1*.

55. "Statement on Nuclear Weapons by International Generals and Admirals," 5 December 1996, http://www.nuclearfiles.org/menu/key-issues/ethics/issues/military/statement-by-international-generals.htm; Les Aspin, "From Deterrence to Denuking: Dealing with Proliferation in the 1990s," *Shaping a Nuclear Policy for the 1990s: A Compendium of Views*, Report of the Defense Policy Panel of the Committee on Armed Services, House of Representatives, One Hundred Second Congress, Second Session Washington, DC, GPO, 1993.

56. Bill Clinton, "Statement by the President," Office of the Press Secretary, The White House, March 6, 2000, available from *www.acronym.org.uk/dd/dd44/44clin.htm*.

57. See William J. Perry, Brent Scowcroft, and Charles D. Ferguson, "US Nuclear Weapons Policy," Independent Task Force

Report No. 62, Washington, DC: Council on Foreign Relations, 2009, p. 16; Nolan, pp. 59-62. One might also note the words of Edward Warner, Assistant Secretary of Strategy and Defense during President Clinton's second term:

> . . . reductions will continue to be a primary objective of the United States. However, for the foreseeable future, we will continue to need a reliable and flexible nuclear deterrent—albeit at lower force levels. . . . Our nuclear posture contributes substantially to our ability to deter any future hostile political leadership with access to nuclear weapons or other weapons of mass destruction against the United States, its forces abroad, its allies, and friends.

See Edward Warner, "Testimony before the Senate Armed Services Subcommittee on Strategic Forces," April 1, 1998, available from *www.fas.org/irp/offdocs/pdd/pdd-60-dd1402.htm*.

58. However, it is also possible that Cohen's statement was influenced by domestic political considerations.

59. See Stephen S. Rosenfeld, "Still on a Cold War Footing," *Washington Post*, October 31, 1997. These officials included John Bolton, Under Secretary of State for Arms Control and International Security; Stephen Cambone, who held various posts in the Department of Defense (DoD) starting in January 2001; Robert Joseph, who served at both the National Security Council and Department of State; and Keith Payne, who served in the DoD.

60. Walker, "Nuclear Enlightenment and Counter-enlightenment," pp. 439-440.

61. Dimitri Simes, "Losing Russia," *Foreign Affairs*, Vol. 86, No. 6, 2007; "Russian General Calls Americans 'Evil'," *UPI*, November 13, 2007, available from *www.upi.com/NewsTrack/Top_News/2007/11/13/russian_general_calls_americans_evil/6480/*; Keith Payne, "The Nuclear Posture Review: Setting the Record Straight," *The Washington Quarterly*, Vol. 28, No. 3, 2005; Charles L. Glaser and Steve Fetter, "National Missile Defense and the Future of U.S. Nuclear Weapons Policy," *International Security*, Vol. 26, No. 1, 2001; U.S. Department of State, "ABM Treaty Fact

Sheet," December 13, 2001, available from *www.state.gov/t/ac/rls/ fs/2001/6848.htm*; Condoleeza Rice, "Promoting the National Interest," *Foreign Affairs*, Vol. 79, No. 1, 2000, p. 59.

62. One counterargument that has been offered with respect to this point is that while the SORT Treaty had no verification provisions, these were already provided for under the START agreement and, as such, were unnecessary. The first half of this argument is stronger than the second, since START-I was set to expire in December 2009 absent conclusion of a START follow-on, and no real effort was made by the Bush administration to negotiate such a deal.

63. Krepon, "Ban the Bomb," pp. 91-92.

64. The "new triad" consists of nuclear (the old triad) and precision non-nuclear strike forces, passive and active defenses (e.g., missile defense, intelligence, and warning systems), and a revitalized defense infrastructure (e.g., the means to produce weapons and detections systems). See "Nuclear Posture Review," Washington, DC: U.S. Department of Defense, December 2001, available from *www.defense.gov/news/jan2002/d20020109npr.pdf*.

65. Payne, "The Nuclear Posture Review."

66. See James R. Schlesinger *et al.*, "Report of the Secretary of Defense Task Force on DoD Nuclear Weapons Management, Phase II: Review of the DoD Nuclear Mission," Washington, DC, December 2008, pp. 7-8. One of the 2001 NPR's goals was to strengthen the credibility of the U.S. nuclear deterrent, which the Bush administration viewed as essential to nuclear nonproliferation. See Samuel W. Bodman and Robert M. Gates, "National Security and Nuclear Weapons in the 21st Century," Washington, DC, 2008, available from *www.defense.gov/news/nuclearweaponspolicy.pdf*; Payne, "The Nuclear Posture Review," p. 146.

67. Some have suggested, however, that increased U.S. conventional capabilities might actually increase the incentives of weaker states to acquire and maintain nuclear arsenals.

68. Stephen Rademaker, "Statement on Confronting Today's Threats, in the First Committee of the General Assembly," New

York, United States Mission to the United Nations, October 3, 2005, p. 4, available from *www.nti.org/e_research/official_docs/dos/dos100305rademaker.pdf*.

69. Walker, "Nuclear Enlightenment and Counter-enlightenment"; John Simpson and Jenny Nielsen, "The 2005 NPT Review Conference: Mission Impossible?" *The Nonproliferation Review*, Vol. 12, No. 2, 2005.

70. See Perkovich and Acton; Patricia Lewis, "Verification, Compliance, and Enforcement," in Perkovich and Acton. This rejection, a type of inversion of the Reagan-era mantra "trust but verify," is particularly interesting because of its internally contradictory nature; at once, it suggests that trust is the bedrock of agreements, while also suggesting that verification is worthless because one cannot trust one's partners.

71. Walker, "Nuclear Enlightenment and Counter-enlightenment"; Sharon Squassoni, "U.S. Nuclear Cooperation with India: Issues for Congress," *CRS Report for Congress*, Washington, DC: Congressional Research Service, October 4, 2006.

72. William C. Potter, "India and the New Look of US Nonproliferation Policy," *The Nonproliferation Review*, Vol. 12, No. 2, 2005, p. 343.

73. Dmitri Trenin, "Russian Perspectives on the Global Elimination of Nuclear Weapons," in Barry Blechman, ed., *Russia and the United States*, Washington, DC: Henry L. Stimson Center, 2009.

74. See Schultz *et al.*, "A World Free of Nuclear Weapons." See also George P. Schultz *et al.*, "How to Protect Our Nuclear Deterrent," *Wall Street Journal*, January 19, 2010; George P. Schultz *et al.*, "Toward a Nuclear-Free World," *Wall Street Journal*, January 15, 2008.

75. A particularly intense contrast of two hawkish figures vis-à-vis the nuclear question is evident between William F. Buckley and Paul Nitze. Buckley would famously scribe that he preferred the "*chance* of being dead" to "the certainty of being Red." Nitze, however, held a moral revulsion toward nuclear weapons, one that both early on and late in life led him to prefer a conventional

force buildup to a nuclear one. See Nitze, "A Threat Mostly to Ourselves"; William F. Buckley, "On Dead-Red," *National Review*, November 17, 1962. See also Tannenwald, "Stigmatizing the Bomb."

76. See, for example, Goodpaster *et al.*

77. Schultz *et al.*, "Toward a Nuclear-Free World"; Schultz *et al.*, "A World Free of Nuclear Weapons.

78. William J. Broad and David E. Sanger, "Obama's Youth Shaped His Nuclear-Free Vision," *New York Times*, July 5, 2009, available from *www.nytimes.com/2009/07/05/world/05nuclear.html*; William Walker, "President-Elect Obama and Nuclear Disarmament: Between Elimination and Restraint," Paris, France: Institut Français des Relations Internationales, Winter 2009.

79. Barack Obama, "Remarks by President Barack Obama, Hradcany Square," Prague, Czech Republic, April 5, 2009, available from *www.whitehouse.gov/the_press_office/Remarks-By-President-Barack-Obama-In-Prague-As-Delivered/*.

80. Ido Daalder and Jan Lodal, "The Logic of Zero: Toward a World Without Nuclear Weapons," *Foreign Affairs*, Vol. 87, No. 6, 2008; Schultz *et al.*, "Toward a Nuclear-Free World."

81. James Acton, "Nuclear Power, Disarmament, and Technological Restraint," *Survival*, Vol. 51, No. 4, 2009.

82. Perry, Scowcroft, and Ferguson, pp. 18-19.

83. Louis Charbonneau and Matt Spetalnick, "U.N. Calls for Nuclear Disarmament, Obama Presides," *Reuters*, September, 24 2009, available from *www.reuters.com/assets/print?aid=USTRE58M0VN20090925*.

84. Paul Richter, "Obama's Nuclear-Free Vision Mired in Debate," *Los Angeles Times*, January 4, 2010, available from *www.latimes.com/news/nation-and-world/la-na-obama-nuclear4-2010jan04,0,1799502.story*.

85. "Nuclear Security Summit 1 Year Anniversary," Washington, DC: Center for Arms Control and Nonproliferation, April 11, 2011, available from *armscontrolcenter.org/policy/nuclearterrorism/articles/nuclear_security_summit_1_year/*.

86. Deepthi Choubey, "Understanding the 2010 NPT Review Conference," Washington, DC: Carnegie Endowment for International Peace, June 3, 2010; Paul K. Kerr *et al.*, "2010 Non-Proliferation Treaty (NPT) Review Conference: Key Issues and Implications," *CRS Report for Congress*, Washington, DC: Congressional Research Service, May 3, 2010; William C. Potter *et al.*, "The 2010 NPT Review Conference: Deconstructing Consensus," *CNS Special Report*, Washington, DC: James Martin Center for Nonproliferation Studies, June 17, 2010.

87. Obama.

88. Freedman, "A New Theory for Nuclear Disarmament," p. 22.

89. Hugh Gusterson, "Narrating Abolition," *Bulletin of the Atomic Scientists*, Vol. 65, No. 3, 2009, p. 15.

90. *Ibid.*

91. See Freedman, "A New Theory for Nuclear Disarmament," p. 26. The problems of nuclear blackmail and virtual arsenals are but two concerns when one plans strategy at extremely low numbers of nuclear weapons or in a nuclear-free world.

92. Perkovich and Acton; Cf. Frank Miller, "Disarmament and Deterrence: A Practitioner's View," in Perkovich and Acton.

93. See, for example, Jon Kyl and Richard Perle, "Our Decaying Nuclear Deterrent," *Wall Street Journal*, June, 30 2009, available from *online.wsj.com/article/SB124623202363966157.html*.

94. Obama.

95. Joseph Biden, "The President's Nuclear Vision," *Wall Street Journal*, January 29, 2010, available from *online.wsj.com/article/SB10001424052748704878904575031382215508268.html*.

96. "Budget of the United States Government, Fiscal Year 2012: 'Department of Energy'," Washington, DC: U.S. Department of Energy, 2012, available from *www.whitehouse.gov/sites/default/files/omb/budget/fy2012/assets/energy.pdf*; Martin Matishak, "Nuclear Agency Officials Warn Against Proposed Spending Cuts," *Global Security Newswire*, March 31, 2011, available from *www.globalsecuritynewswire.org/gsn/nw_20110331_3274.php*; "Obama to Seek \$5B Nuclear-Weapon Complex Spending Boost," *Global Security Newswire*, January 29, 2010, available from *gsn.nti.org/gsn/nw_20100129_1187.php*; Martin Matishak, "Obama Requests \$11 Billion for Nuclear Agency," *Global Security Newswire*, February 2, 2010, available from *gsn.nti.org/gsn/nw_20100202_8450.php*; Schultz *et al.*, "How to Protect Our Nuclear Deterrent"; William J. Perry *et al.*, "America's Strategic Posture: The Final Report of the Congressional Commission on the Strategic Posture of the United States," Washington, DC: United States Institute of Peace, May 2008.

97. Ellen Tauscher, "Remarks to U.S. Strategic Command Deterrence Symposium, U.S. Strategic Command," Omaha, Nebraska, July 30, 2009, available from *www.acronym.org.uk/docs/0907/doc11.htm*.

98. *Quadrennial Defense Review Report*, Washington, DC: US Department of Defense, February 2010, p. 14, available from *www.defense.gov/qdr/images/QDR_as_of_12Feb10_1000.pdf*.

99. Hans M. Kristensen, Robert S. Norris, and Ivan Oelrich, "From Counterforce to Minimal Deterrence: A New Nuclear Policy on the Path Toward Eliminating Nuclear Weapons," Occasional Paper No. 7, Washington, DC: Federation of American Scientists and the Natural Resources Defense Council, April 2009, pp. 15-18.

100. There are a limited number of efforts in this direction, including James Acton's work on stability at low numbers. See James Acton, *Deterrence During Disarmament: Deep Nuclear Reductions and International Security*, Vol. 417, Adelphi Paper, New York: Routledge, 2011.

101. Stephen I. Schwartz and Deepti Choubey, *Nuclear Security Spending: Assessing Costs, Examining Priorities*, Washington, DC: Carnegie Endowment for International Peace, 2009, pp. 6-7.

102. "Budget of the United States Government, Fiscal Year 2012: 'Department of Energy'"; Matishak, "Nuclear Agency Officials Warn Against Proposed Spending Cuts"; "Obama to Seek $5B Nuclear-Weapon Complex Spending Boost"; Matishak, "Obama Requests $11 Billion for Nuclear Agency."

103. Schultz *et al.*, "How to Protect Our Nuclear Deterrent"; Perry *et al.*, "America's Strategic Posture: The Final Report of the Congressional Commission on the Strategic Posture of the United States"; James R. Schlesinger *et al.*, "Report of the Secretary of Defense Task Force on DoD Nuclear Weapons Management, Phase I: The Air Force's Nuclear Mission," December 2008; Schlesinger *et al.*, "Report of the Secretary of Defense Task Force on DoD Nuclear Weapons Management, Phase II: Review of the DoD Nuclear Mission."

104. Matthew Evangelista, "Nuclear Abolition or Nuclear Umbrella? Choices and Contradictions in Proposals for 'Global Zero'," Unpublished Manuscript, July 2009, p. 7; Janne E. Nolan and James R. Holmes, "The Bureaucracy of Deterrence," *Bulletin of the Atomic Scientists*, Vol. 64, No. 1, 2008; Graham Allison and Philip Zelikow, *Essence of Decision: Explaining the Cuban Missile Crisis*, 2nd Ed., New York: Longman, 1999.

105. Indeed, career DoD officials actively sought to exclude arms control "weirdos" from the process of crafting the 1994 NPR. See Nolan and Holmes, "The Bureaucracy of Deterrence," p. 42; Nolan.

106. "Clashes Seen Over Obama's Disarmament Goals," *Global Security Newswire*, January 4, 2010, available from *gsn.nti.org/gsn/nw_20100104_2405.php*.

107. Lawrence Freedman, "Nuclear Disarmament: From a Popular Movement to an Elite Project, and Back Again?" in Perkovich and Acton; Krepon, "Ban the Bomb."

108. See Steven Kull *et al.*, "Americans and Russians on International Security and Arms Control Questionnaire," PIPA/Knowledge Network, January 2008, p. 9, available from *www.cissm.umd.edu/papers/files/cissm_jan08_quaire.pdf*. More recently, the

general public showed tepid interest—at best—over the fate of New START, despite months of intense political fights over ratification.

109. *Ibid.*; Knopf; David Cortright, *Peace Works: The Citizen's Role in Ending the Cold War*, Boulder, CO: Westview, 1993; David S. Meyer, *A Winter of Discontent: The Nuclear Freeze and American Politics*, Boulder, CO: Praeger, 1990.

110. Kingston Rief, "House Armed Services Committee Toys With American Security," Washington, DC: Center for Arms Control & Nonproliferation: Nukes of Hazard, May 12, 2011, available from *nukesofhazardblog.com/story/2011/5/12/15843/5281*.

111. Broad and Sanger.

112. *Quadrennial Defense Review Report*, p. 14.

113. Schultz *et al.*, "How to Protect Our Nuclear Deterrent."

114. Angela Charlton, "Disarmament Talks Strained Over Mideast, Russia," *The Washington Post*, February 2, 2010; "Disarmament Summit Focuses on Russia, Middle East," *Global Security Newswire*, February 3, 2010; Martin Matishak, "U.S. Should Embrace Using Nukes for Nuclear Threat Only, Experts Say," *Global Security Newswire*, January 25, 2010, available from *gsn.nti.org/site-services/print_friendly.php?ID=nw_20100125_3469*; Trenin.

115. Acton, "Nuclear Power, Disarmament, and Technological Restraint."

116. Alexander H. Rothman and Lawrence J. Korb, "Pakistan doubles its nuclear arsenal: Is it time to start worrying?" *Bulletin of the Atomic Scientists*, 2011.

117. Charlton, "Disarmament Talks Strained Over Mideast, Russia"; Isabelle Lasserre, "Désarmement nucléaire: Paris résiste à 'l'option zéro'" ("Nuclear Disarmament: Paris Resists 'Zero Option'") *Le Figaro*, February 3, 2010, available from *www.lefigaro.fr/international/2010/02/03/01003-20100203ARTFIG00443-desarmement-nucleaire-paris-resiste-a-l-option-zero-.php*; Natalie Nougayrède, "Paris réticent face à l'élimination de l'arme nucléaire"

("Paris Reluctant to Eliminate Nuclear Weapons") *Le Monde*, February 4, 2010, available from *www.lemonde.fr/organisations-internationales/article/2010/02/02/paris-reticent-face-a-l-elimination-de-l-arme-nucleaire_1300050_3220.html*.

118. This paradox has been noted by a wide array of former policymakers, including William Cohen, Keith Payne, and Mikhail Gorbachev. See "U.S. Military Power Could Hinder Nuclear Disarmament Goals," *Global Security Newswire*, April 17, 2009, available from *www.globalsecuritynewswire.org/gsn/nw_20090417_5439.php*; Payne, p. 146; Nolan, p. 2.

119. Evangelista, pp. 3-4.

120. Lewis.

121. The confidence of allies in U.S. extended deterrent guarantees is critical if one accepts the conventional wisdom that these guarantees have helped convince states such as Japan to forego nuclear weapons, a topic of debate that is beyond the scope of this article. With respect to conventional prompt global strike antagonizing potential peer competitors or weaker states, one of the key issues to consider is the difficulty of distinguishing between defensive conventional global strike forces and offensive nuclear forces.

www.ingramcontent.com/pod-product-compliance
Lightning Source LLC
Chambersburg PA
CBHW070624290526
45790CB00002B/989